Countries

Canada

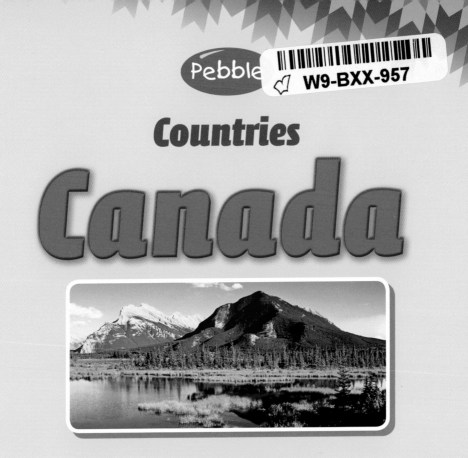

by Christine Juarez

Consulting Editor: Gail Saunders-Smith, PhD

CAPSTONE PRESS
a capstone imprint

Pebble Books are published by Capstone Press,
1710 Roe Crest Drive, North Mankato, Minnesota 56003
www.capstonepub.com

Library of Congress Cataloging-in-Publication Data
Juarez, Christine, 1976–
Canada / by Christine Juarez.
     pages cm.—(Pebble books. Countries)
Includes bibliographical references and index.
Summary: "Simple text and full-color photographs illustrate the land, animals, and people of
Canada"—Provided by publisher.
ISBN 978-1-4765-3515-9 (paperback)
1. Canada—Juvenile literature. I. Title.
F1008.2.J83 2014
971—dc23
                                                                    2013002011

Editorial Credits
Erika L. Shores, editor; Bobbie Nuytten, designer; Wanda Winch, media researcher;
Jennifer Walker, production specialist

Photo Credits
Capstone, 4, 22 (currency); Dreamstime: Fallsview, 19, Lijuan Guo, 15; Shutterstock: Elena
Elisseeva, 22 (flag), gary718, 5, Henk Jacobs, 13, Mark Skalny, 11, Nelu Goia, cover, Ohmega1982,
back cover (globe), outdoorsman, 9, Regien Paassen, 17, Silvia Popa, cover, 1 (design element),
Sven Hoppe, 21, TTphoto, 1, 7

Note to Parents and Teachers

The Countries set supports national social studies standards related to
people, places, and culture. This book describes and illustrates Canada.
The images support early readers in understanding the text. The repetition
of words and phrases helps early readers learn new words. This book
also introduces early readers to subject-specific vocabulary words, which
are defined in the Glossary section. Early readers may need assistance to
read some words and to use the Table of Contents, Glossary, Read More,
Internet Sites, and Index sections of the book.

Printed in the United States of America in North Mankato, Minnesota.
122016   010206R

Table of Contents

Where Is Canada?

Canada is the second-largest country in the world. Canada is in North America. Its capital is Ottawa.

CANADA

★ Ottawa

Landforms

Lakes and forests are found throughout Canada. Frozen land called tundra is in northern Canada. Mountains, plains, and farmland cover southern Canada.

Animals

The tundra is home to polar bears and caribou. Canada geese and loons spend the summer in Canada's lakes.

Language and Population

More than 34 million people live in Canada. Most people live in cities in southern Canada. English and French are the country's official languages.

Food

Canadians eat seafood, meat, and vegetables. Poutine is a popular dish made of French fries, cheese, and gravy. Most of the world's maple syrup comes from Canada.

Sap from a maple tree drips into a bucket. People use the sap to make maple syrup.

Celebrations

Canadians celebrate Canada Day on July 1. This holiday marks when Canada became a country. People celebrate with parties, music, and fireworks.

Where People Work

Most Canadians work in service jobs in tourism, schools, and hospitals. Farmers grow wheat and barley. Miners dig for metals such as gold and iron.

A special bus brings tourists to Canada's Columbia Icefields.

Transportation

Canadians have many ways to travel. They can take cars, buses, trains, or airplanes. In the far north, people use skis and snowmobiles.

Famous Sport

Ice hockey is Canada's most popular sport. Canadians invented the game in the late 1800s. People watch and play ice hockey year-round in Canada.

Country Facts

Name: Canada

Capital: Ottawa

Population: 34,568,211 (July 2013 estimate)

Size: 3,855,103 square miles
(9,984,671 square kilometers)

Languages: English and French

Main Crops: wheat, barley, fruits, vegetables

Money:
Canadian dollar

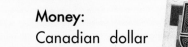

Canada's flag

Glossary

Canada goose—a common wild goose with a black neck and head

capital—the city in a country where the government is based

caribou—a large North American mammal that looks like a deer

hockey—a game played on ice with a stick and a puck

language—the way people speak or talk

North America—the continent that includes the United States, Canada, Mexico, and Central America

official—having the approval of a country or a certain group of people

plain—a large, flat area of land

popular—liked or enjoyed by many people

snowmobile—a vehicle with an engine and skis or runners; snowmobiles travel over snow

tourism—the business of providing entertainment, food, and hotels for travelers

tundra—a large plain that is frozen most of the year; no trees grow on the tundra

Read More

Kalman, Bobbie. *Canada: The Land*. The Lands, Peoples, and Cultures Series. New York: Crabtree, 2010.

McMillan, Sue. *Find Out about Canada*. Hauppauge, N.Y.: Barron's Educational Series, 2009.

Sexton, Colleen. *Canada*. Exploring Countries. Minneapolis: Bellwether Media, 2011.

Internet Sites

FactHound offers a safe, fun way to find Internet sites related to this book. All of the sites on FactHound have been researched by our staff.

Here's all you do:
Visit *www.facthound.com*
Type in this code: 9781476530758

Super-cool stuff!

Check out projects, games and lots more at
www.capstonekids.com

Index